THE SECRET TO NAIL THE COMPETENCY BASED INTERVIEW

What You Need To Know

Blessing N. Ikiseh

Bibieandrea Services Venture

Copyright © 2021 Blessing Nkechi Ikiseh

No form of this publication should be reproduced, distributed, transmitted or reprinted in any form or by any means, including photocopying, recording, or other electronic or mechanical methods, without the express written permission from the author, except in the case of brief quotations embodied in critical reviews and certain other noncommercial uses permitted by copyright law. Violation and copyright of this manual are punishable by law. Anyone caught in the act of copywriting and reproducing this material without the author's permission will be prosecuted.

Plagiarism is not accepted in any form, ensure you are familiar with the regulations on plagiarism. Severe penalties are imposed for plagiarizing this work, so you mustn't blatantly or inadvertently copy this project without properly citing and referencing the author.

DISCLAIMER:
The content published in this document is solely for educational, illustrative and informational purposes, with no intent to falsely characterize, recommend or injure any name, organization and/or business entity.

This project is dedicated to God Almighty for his never-ending mercies, insights, guidance and support. Also, to my parents, Mr. Christopher Ikechukwu Ikiseh and Mrs. Anthonia Ifeayinwa Ikiseh.

Chance favours the prepared mind! Nobody is responsible for your interview mistakes - only you are.

BLESSING NKECHI IKISEH

CONTENTS

Title Page
Copyright
Dedication
Epigraph
Foreword
Introduction
Preface
DECLARATION

THE SECRET TO NAIL THE COMPETENCY BASED INTERVIEW	1
Abstract	3
CHAPTER ONE	5
Pros and Cons of CompetencY based Interview	7
CHAPTER TWO	9
TYPES OF COMPETENCY-BASED QUESTIONS	10
CHAPTER THREE	15
THIRTY MOST COMMON COMPETENCY-BASED INTERVIEW QUESTIONS	19
CHAPTER FOUR	22
Types of Questions	24
Shine with StAR	28
Use 'power words' in your Applications/CV/Resume	30

WHO USES ATS'S AND HOW TO SPOT THEM	32
Dealing with gaps	35
Personal Statements	37
Tricks Recruiters use to filter Applications	39
HOW TO HANDLE REJECTIONS	41
CHAPTER FIVE	43
THE COMPETENCY-BASED INTERVIEW Q&A	44
CHAPTER SUMMARY	62
RECOMMENDATION	64
PRACTICE THE FOLLOWING QUESTIONS	66
Other Questions To Look Out For	70
twenty-five Top Transferable Skills	75
APPENDIX	77
Epilogue	79
Afterword	81
THE JOB DESCRIPTION IS A CRY FOR HELP	83
SURVIVING THE GLOBAL PANDEMIC: COVID HACKS TO STAYING MOTIVATED & ENCOURAGED	85
MOTIVATION	89
Acknowledgement	91
About The Author	93
Books By This Author	95
Praise For Author	97
TESTIMONIAL	99
ABOUT BIBIEANDREA SERVICES VENTURE	103
Our Services	105

FOREWORD

This book has been carefully written to assist professionals while facing the competency-based interview. I recommend *'The Secret To Nail The Competency-based Interview: What You Need To Know'* to all professionals who are finding it hard to nail the competency-based interview and to inspire confidence in them. It is no longer news that big companies like IBM, Facebook, Google, LinkedIn, to mention a few, rely on the competency-based interview to select candidates. It is with this fact, the book draws from my personal experience to help professionals realise the fullness of their potential.

INTRODUCTION

How can you give the answer an employer is looking for, when you cannot identify or know the question you are likely to get asked?

It is no longer news that successful companies/businesses rely on the competency-based interview technique. The interview can be stressful and nerve-wracking, if you do your homework, prepare, research and practice common competencies questions, there is every chance you will land your dream job. This is what the book will teach you.

The book will walk you through the process of answering the competency-based interview questions with real-life and hands-on examples. Also, this book will teach you how to structure your competency-based interview answer using positive indicators to tell a compelling story.

After studying this book, you will better understand the competency-based interview and the basic application principles.

PREFACE

The job interview is a two-way street, when done right, can turn into an engaging conversation between the candidate and the interviewer(s), and by this, you will be one step ahead of your peers.

In my 12 years of experience as an HR Practitioner/Recruiter, I have learned that even the most qualified and exceptional candidate fails to stand-out in the competency-based interview. This fact birthed **'The Secret To Nail The Competency-based Interview: What You Need To Know'**. The book is written to inspire confidence among professionals while facing the interview world.

DECLARATION

This project is the result of my own independent work/investigation, except where otherwise stated.

COMPETENCY BASED INTERVIEW

THE SECRET TO NAIL THE COMPETENCY BASED INTERVIEW

© Blessing N. Ikiseh 2021

All rights reserved. No part of this publication may be reproduced, stored in a retrieval system or transmitted in any form or by any means, electronic, mechanical, photocopying, recording or otherwise, without the prior permission in writing from the author.

Editors

Blessing N. Ikiseh & Kit Gerard Grant.

08022372183

bibieandrea@gmail.com

ABSTRACT

The interview can be nerve-wracking, and some things do not change as many employers still rely on competency-based interview questions. The author has learned that even the most qualified and exceptional candidates fail to stand-out in the competency-based interview. This fact birthed the Secret to Nail the Competency-based Interview: What you need to know. This book is written to inspire confidence among professionals, while facing the interview world.

The book discussed at length the competency-based interview, its meaning and the types of competencies being accessed, while citing real-life and hands-on experience – drawing inference from the author's experiences. It explained the pros and cons of the competency-based interview and how competencies are scored, both positive and negative indicators. Last of all, the book also focused at length, the basic principles of the job application process, giving relevance to ATSs and how to spot them; personal statements; how to handle rejections; types of questions and the thirty (30) most common competency-based interview questions.

After studying this book, you will better understand the competency-based interview.

Competency-based interview questions always require something you have done in the past.

CHAPTER ONE

THE COMPETENCY BASED INTERVIEW

The Interview can be nerve-wracking, and some things do not change as many employers still rely on competency-based interview questions. This Book is going to compile the 30 questions you are most likely to get asked and a handy trick for nailing your answer and other relevant things you need to know about the job interview and application tricks. How can you answer what an employer is looking for when you cannot identify or know the questions you are likely to get asked?

The Chartered Institute of Personnel Development (CIPD) defined **"Competencies as the behaviour employees must input into a situation in order to achieve high levels of performance"**.

Competency-based interview questions are designed to let you talk; they are open and they invite you to respond, telling the employer about a real-life challenge that you have faced. Competency questions help employers understand how you have previously dealt with specific situations, tasks or people, revealing the past behaviour you used to resolve a specific situation. Many employers believed that past behaviour or experience used in resolving a situation by an employee is the best indicator to predict future performance.

The competency-based method to interviewing will learn about your background and experience relevant to the competencies being accessed. Competency-based questions let you give specific examples of times when you have demonstrated the skills required for the position/role. Avoid being vague, and don't waste space writing about skills you have that aren't relevant to the job applied for.

There are several types of competency-based questions you can be asked including technical skills, behaviours and knowledge.

Competency questions focus on finding specific skills that are important to that job. A competency-based interview is also known as situation-based interview questions. For example, an interviewer(s) may ask you about your communication skill. They can also ask you to give an example when you used verbal communication to solve a work-related problem.

PROS AND CONS OF COMPETENCY BASED INTERVIEW

Employers often use a set of scripts for competency-based interviews. This script is paired with a score-based technique for assessing candidates. Competency-based questions require job applicants to recall their personal experiences. When interviewing candidates, employers are mostly looking for two things:

1. Someone who can excel at doing the job and;
2. Someone who can work well with existing employees.

Competency-based interview questions give candidates every chance/opportunity to show they have all the experience and skills necessary to perform on the job. Competency-based interview questions always require an example of something you have done in the past.

Cons Of Competency-Based Interview

How to tell you are being asked a competency-based interview question?

If the employer doesn't mention that they are about to ask you competency-based questions, you can pick them out by the way the question is phrased. Competency-based questions typically lead you towards describing a situation and task. For example, an employer may start the question by asking:

- Tell me about a time when you solved a problem?
- Give an example of when you dealt with a difficult customer?
- Describe a time when you used technical skill to resolve a conflict?
- Have you ever been in a situation where you had to beat the deadline in a team?

How can you answer these questions if you are not prepared? This is what the handbook is about. It will walk you through the process of answering the competency-based interview questions with real-life and hands-on examples.

CHAPTER TWO

CHAPTER INTRODUCTION

After studying this chapter, you will better understand how to answer the competency-based Interview questions.

See you in the next section!

TYPES OF COMPETENCY-BASED QUESTIONS

Using the STAR Technique/method to answering the competency-based interview questions, this section will walk you through the process and everything you need to know about nailing competency-based interview questions. Also, it will show you the difference between the STAR, CARL and PARL Model/technique to answering the Competency-based interview questions.

It is no longer news that successfully businesses/companies like Google, Facebook, IBM, etc. rely on competency-based interview techniques. The interview can be stressful and nerve-wracking, if you do your homework, prepare, research and practice common competencies questions, there is every chance you will land your dream job.

There are three types of competency-based or behavioural interview questions. They include:

1. The CARL Model
2. The P.A.R.L Model and
3. The STAR Technique

The C.a.r.l Technique In Answering The Behavioural Interview Questions.

C.A.R.L stands for:

- → C = Context
- → A = Action
- → R = Result
- → L = Learning

The C.A.R.L Technique is used to answer competency-based interview questions that are results and learning-oriented. For instance, you can be asked a question like tell me a time you made a mistake at work and what did you learn from your mistake and how are you applying the lessons learned in your current work? You use the C.A.R.L technique to answer this question.

You can use the *P.A.R.L model* to answer behavioural interview questions that are problem-oriented. For example, you can be asked a question like tell me a time you encountered disagreement at work with a team and how did you handle it? And/or tell me a time you had a conflict at work and what did you do to solve the problem.

P.A.R.L stand for:

- → P = Problem
- → A = Action
- → R = Result
- → L = Learning

Now that you know the difference between the C.A.R.L technique and PARL method to answering the competency-based or behavioural interview questions, you should start applying them to your advantage. Properly structure your answer to fit around your previous or current job role.

The next section will be looking at the STAR method to Competency-based Interview questions in more detail.

An interviewer might also ask you to give an example of the time you have used five types of skills to solve a problem or a difficult situation. You may be wondering how to do this? To do this, you need to be prepared, memorize and practice some key competency examples that you can adapt based on the question asked. The author will explain exactly how to do this in a later topic/session of this handbook.

When preparing for a competency-based interview, the following three steps are recommended:
- Find out what competencies the employer is looking for.
- Identify the competency question examples.
- Develop a compelling story for each competency.

At the interview, pick the right story for the right question.

Competencies are the knowledge, skills, capabilities and behaviours that are necessary to be successful in a given job. But a candidate can anticipate what types are likely to be asked in an interview if they are familiar with the job they are applying for.

- Start with the job ad.
- Read the role description.
- Look for keywords that match the competencies sought after by the employer.
- Most bullet points in the ad will equate a competency.
- Search online for articles that describe the role.
- Search for the job title followed by the job description.

For example, a project manager job description will spell out the requisite skills and competencies in the job ad. Most employers will require a blend of technical, situational and behavioural skill sets. If the job ad specifically mentions these mixtures of skills, prepare competency answers for all three areas. For each competency you know the employer is looking for, find an example from your work or education history that demonstrates you possess the skills.

Prepare competency question examples that are positive, showing off your past successes and above all, explain how you have brought or added value to your previous employer(s) with measurable results.

If you struggle to come up with a compelling story from your experience, speak with friends and family or an expert in the field and ask them when they have seen you behaved or used that specific skill.

The best recommendation is to structure each example using the STAR Technique.

The STAR Technique or method stands for:

→ S = Situation
→ T = TASK
→ A = Action

→ R = Result

Situation. Setting the scene to the example that you are giving, also known as the introduction to your compelling story.

Task. This means describing or throwing more light on what you wanted to achieve (task).

Action. This includes communicating what you did.

Result. Describing the action steps you took while discussing the result – how the situation was resolved.

In chapter three, we are going to be looking at the competency-based scoring measures both positive and negative indicators in more detail.

See you in the next slide.

CHAPTER THREE

THE SCORING INDICATOR

This chapter will focus on the scoring indicators used by employers to score your competency-based answers.

For STAR based or situation-based questions, you split your answer into four (4):

- Situation: This describes the background or context of the job.
- Task: The challenge you were faced with.
- Action: Explain the steps you took, how and why you did it.
- Result: Describes how the job ended, what you accomplished and what you learned from the situation.

How competency-based questions are scored, both positive and negative indicators will now be explained.

Positive And Negative Indicators

This relates to or describes the problem or situation you have encountered.

Employers want to see that you can give evidence as to why you have certain strengths or capabilities. When describing or practising your STAR interview answer, don't spend too long describing the situation or task – structure your answer. The situation is all about setting the scene and describing the context of the story. Use one or two sentences to describe the employer you worked for in your past or recent job, the role (e.g. human resource manager), and any relevant background information. In a short sentence, describe the problem or challenge you or your employer faced, and the goal you were working towards. Explain to the employer why this task is relevant to the role you are applying for.

Focus on what you did to resolve the situation or how you measured success with key results.

1. Describe who else you worked with during the process
2. The steps you took
3. The challenges encountered
4. The specific skills you used to be successful
5. Describe the outcome. This should be positive
6. Emphasize the action steps you took that led to the result

Results are best evidenced by numbers. Express how you delivered value for the employer.

Many employers judge the quality of a candidate competency interview answers using a scale or scorecard. Several employers will handle scoring differently, depending on their criteria. Some measure using a scale of 1 - 5 and others will score you with a scorecard of 1 - 10.

Typically, you will be judged on positive and negative indicators, which will be to score high, you will need to show the following:

- How you dealt with the problem positively
- How you compromised
- Your willingness to learn: You need to show a willingness to accept help and grow from the experience
- How you handle pressure
- How you see challenges as problems
- How you tried to solve the problem alone and failed
- Whether you cracked under pressure
- Your negative attitude to the solution: These are what shouldn't come out as your answer. Learn to structure your answer with positivity or using positive indicators.

Scoring Measure

This is how the interviewer(s) or trained judges will score your answers.

1. Did you demonstrate or show the required experience in your answer?
2. Are your examples relevant to the job?
3. How you articulated your role, the action and your contribution to the outcomes or result?

In summary, the STAR Technique stands for Situation, Task, Action and Result.

In answering the competency-based interview questions, this method is necessary for success. This model is used to answer the competency-based interview that is situation-based.

C.A.R.L Stands for Context, Action, Result and Learning.

The C.A.R.L technique is used to answer the competency-based interview that is results and learning-oriented.

The P.A.R.L Model stands for *Problem, Action, and Result.*

You can use the PARL technique to answer competency-based questions that are problem-oriented.

THIRTY MOST COMMON COMPETENCY-BASED INTERVIEW QUESTIONS

The Thirty (30) most Common Competency-based Interview Questions are also known as 'transferable skills'.

Below are the likely questions you are going to get asked in an Interview.

Excellent Customer Service	How you have TO lead a team	Leadership style with a group to get the best outcomes
How you beat a deadline or de-	Attention to detail	How you motivate your team or

livered result at a pace		your colleague to achieve success
How you collaborated with your team to bring result	How you dealt with a difficult customer	Resilience
How you made effective decision	Handling a difficult situation or decision	How you manage or resolve conflict-related issues
How you managed a quality service or managed a team	How you accept feedback, change and improved organisational skills	Problem-solving skills
Leading and communicating effectively	Creativity	Passion and energy
Strategic Thinking (e.g. outside the box thinking)	How you managed a situation	Delivering value for money or result
Teamwork/team building	Stakeholder management	Integrity
Your communication skills	Working under Pressure or managing workload	Handling or taking control of a situation
Your Relationship building capability	Your Sales skills	Your flexibility and adaptability skills

Now, we have come to the end of chapter three, the next chapter, will be looking at the basic application principles.

CHAPTER FOUR

BASIC APPLICATION PRINCIPLES

Application forms consist of a blend of (personal details, qualifications, work experience and sections) and other selection criteria, where you will be required to write about yourself in a way that shows or demonstrates your (KSAOs) – Knowledge, Skills, Abilities and other experiences. Besides, write a well-structured and well-argued case in your statement that you are the right person for the job while referring or stressing on the person specification set out in the job advert. To show you are the best candidate for the job role and get an interview, you need to demonstrate personality and confidence because employers have countless job application forms to sift through.

Gather all the relevant information about the details of your academic achievements, employment history and contact information for your referees. Do your research to make a great first impression and find out the purpose, vision, mission and goals of the organisation you're applying for, the industry or sector they operate in and who their main competitors are. You can easily get this information by browsing their social media handles/channels/websites. This is a good place to start.

Understand, study and familiarize yourself with the job description so that you can refer back to the specific skills and qualities the employer is looking out for as you complete the application form. In brief, read the instructions carefully, ensure you complete the correct sections of the application and know the date of the job deadline.

In conclusion, consider your motivation for applying, which includes values, ethics, culture, opportunities for career advancement, size of the organisation, induction and training, research and development, innovation, leadership in their field, flexible working condition or whatever your motivation is for applying.

TYPES OF QUESTIONS

There are several types of questions to look out for during competency-based interviews.

   1. Motivational Questions: Why did you agree to choose the organisation? Do your career goals align with theirs? Are you a 'good fit' and best candidate for the job? Show you have done your research by conveying enthusiasm for the job role.

   2. Strength-based Questions: What kind of work do you enjoy? Your personality traits, behaviour and working style. Learn about the values and the qualities of the organisation. This is relevant to better assist you to position and structure your answer. Example of a strength-based question include: Tell me about your greatest strength?

   3. Evidence-based/Competency/Behavioural Questions: The STAR technique or situational method uses evidence-based scenarios to demonstrate skillsets.

In summary, Motivational Questions include:
- How well you have researched the organisation, passion and

knowledge in the field.
- Why have you decided to apply to the organisation?
- Why are you interested in the job or course?
- The job role and key activities and why these appeal to you.

These questions assess your knowledge of the sector, your current professional development within the job role, and employers looking at the following criteria:

→ Does your background match their needs and the requirement of the job?

You need to thoroughly and thoughtfully research the industry, job role or course and the company to properly structure your answer.

Example of a well-structured answer in an application for a Marketing and Communications Assistant for a local sports association: 'What attracts you to this job? Tell us what makes you suitable'. (Max. 100 words).

> I am excited by the idea of representing the Association in its dealings with the media and local community. I have studied Media Relations as part of my degree and particularly enjoyed researching sports sponsorship in my final year. The position involves using my writing skills which I first developed by producing press statements that secured greater local press coverage for my amateur lacrosse club. Helping to

develop a strong marketing strategy is another attractive feature of the post, as I am fascinated by how different organisations develop and maintain their image. (95 words).

This answer demonstrates the candidate has found out about the role and explained why they find specific elements of the job attractive. It indicates relevant activities that the applicant has got involved with, showing skills and knowledge that would be of relevance to the post.

The answer uses language that demonstrates enthusiasm and interest in this work.

Source: Retrieved from the University of South Wales Careers Connect Event.

Strength-based questions focus on what you enjoy doing rather than what you can do.

Be open and honest, come across as positive and convey a lot of enthusiasm. Consider the following when presenting your answer:

- Academic achievements
- Work experience including extra-curricular activities. Think about what you enjoy and why do you enjoy them; this will make you better understand your strengths and what you want out of a career
- Describe something that you learnt recently

- What does success mean to you?
- Which do you prefer - starting a task or finishing a task?

SHINE WITH STAR

S = *Situation:* Setting the scene to the situation you encountered. Your introductory story.

T = *Task:* The objective of the task that needed to be completed.

A = *Action:* What is your responsibility in completing the task. The actions/duties/skills; your role in the job.

R = *Result:* The outcome of the job you accomplished. This can be negative or positive. If negative, you will need to demonstrate you have reflected and learnt the lessons by showing what you would do differently next time to achieve the desired result.

For Example:

> **Situation**: Whilst acting as a relief supervisor at a well-known pizza restaurant, a customer began to loudly complain about the service being slow.
>
> **Task:** To satisfy the person without upsetting other customers who were also waiting for their food who had arrived earlier.
>
> **Action:** I listened carefully to the 'customers' point of view. Calmly and diplomatically I explained that there was a lack

of staff due to illness. I reassured the customer that the order was being dealt with and offered complimentary drinks whilst waiting.

Result: The customer calmed down and appreciated the situation we faced. They realized that it wasn't deliberate and decided to wait quietly, with the free drinks. I learnt the importance of listening to people and seeing their point of view

Tips for You.

1. Focus on giving employers evidence of a time when you have demonstrated those skills.
2. Focus on what you did and directly highlight the skills you were using/developed.
3. Focus on specific examples and use skills-based language.

Source: Retrieved from the University of South Wales Careers Connect Event

USE 'POWER WORDS' IN YOUR APPLICATIONS/CV/RESUME

Here are a few examples of power words.

Accomplished; Achieved; Adapted; Advised; Analyzed; Co-ordinated; Communicated.

Completed; Created; Delivered; Developed; Enhanced; Established; Fulfilled; Helped.

Implemented; Improved; Influenced; Led; Maintained; Motivated; Negotiated; Organized.

Participated; Persuaded; Planned; Researched;

Resolved; Team Working; Trained.

You have to use short sentences and get to the point, citing examples and evidence to prove your point where appropriate. This makes it easier to read and communicate key selling points relevant to the job or course applied to.

WHO USES ATS'S AND HOW TO SPOT THEM

A TS's go by the name 'Applicant Tracking Systems. It is also known as online application systems, CV scanning software or resume robots. These job tools are used by several employers to vet candidates' CVs/resumes and applications using algorithms and keywords to find the best applicants for the job, prioritizing these for the second round of review.

You can spot these ATS's in Job boards & CV databases including Indeed, Monster, Milkround, Google and CV-Library. Social platforms like LinkedIn and Glassdoor and Recruitment firms such as GradJobs, MichaelPage, Hays and Graduate Recruitment Bureau, etc.

Online Forms

Whenever you are asked to fill in an online form with individual text fields be sure that you are dealing with an ATS. Some systems will ask you to upload your CV, this will be automatically scanned. You may also be asked to paste in the text of your CV manually. Don't be deceived by the latter; your CV text will still be scrutinized by the machine once you hit 'send'. Online forms like these are mostly found on larger company websites, but recruiters and job boards also use them.

One-Click Apply Functions

Several social platforms like LinkedIn and Glassdoor use one-click application functionalities to simplify the application process. LinkedIn's 'Easy Apply' button for example lets you apply for jobs advertised on the platform without sending you to an external page. All you need to supply is your email address, phone number and CV. Once submitted your application goes through an ATS, prioritizing the best and most relevant candidates for the hiring manager based on their CVs as well as the content of their LinkedIn profile

Urls

One of the easiest ways to spot ATS's is to look at the URL. Employers that work with ATS companies will often direct you from their career page to another website which, although carrying their branding, may have the name of the ATS Company in its URL. Names to look out for include: Taleo, Oracle, Jobvite, Workday, SAP SuccessFactors and Hire by Google.

With 98% of Fortune 500 companies using applicant tracking systems, the chances of encountering them during your job search are high. Spotting them is only half the work; your success will ultimately depend on your CV making it through that initial vetting round, so make sure it's fully optimized to take on the machines.

Mastering Applicant Tracking Systems

Use standard fonts such as Arial, Calibri, Georgia, Tahoma or Verdana. Leave out special characters. Do not use headers and footers, tables, graphics and logos. Make sure your headings are clear. For example, use simple headings such as 'Work experience', rather than 'Professional expertise'. Provide the full titles of qualifications or organisations that you have worked for, along with abbreviations or acronyms. For example, The Chartered Institute of Marketing (CIM) - Certificate in Professional Marketing, 2020 - 2021.

Add dates at the end of your qualifications and work experience, rather than at the start. For example, OXY Shop, Nigeria - Part-time Sales Assistant, Sept 2020 - Jun 2021.

DEALING WITH GAPS

Give a concrete reason why there is a gap in your CV/Resume in the application. Here are good examples to follow:

Made redundant from my position as assistant manager in the XYZ store.

❖ ❖ ❖

Explain it in the application.

1. Spent three mornings a week attending the local work club to develop skills in writing applications, interview technique and searching for jobs. Proofread each other's applications and provided positive feedback. Motivated and encouraged each other within the club to apply for jobs and celebrated our success.

2. Completed a part-time basic computing course which included an introduction to web design, computer programming and applications. Developed skills in designing interactive web pages using JavaScript.

3. Volunteered at my son's theatre group and worked as part of a team to design, build and paint stage sets and props for a production of Oliver Twist. It proved a great success and ran for four nights to a full audience. The production made a profit of over £300 allowing the group to continue to rent a room in the local community centres.

PERSONAL STATEMENTS

This section will discuss in detail what to include in your statement and why you have decided to apply for the job. Describe what motivates and attracts you to the job. Show that you have a realistic understanding of what is involved and can draw parallels with positive experiences you have already had, even if these have been in different settings.

Why this organisation?

Say why you want to work for this particular organisation, for example, this might be related to its clients, ethos, reputation or staff development policy. Draw on the research you have done in preparation to apply – don't just make it up! Be honest about your reasons (although don't just say that the salary appeals!) and try to write concisely. Make the match against the job description. State clearly and provide evidence of how you match the job description, using the information you have gathered as part of preparing to apply. This can be an ideal opportunity for you to demonstrate your relevant skills, attributes and specific knowledge. For example, if the job description asks for an experience of teamwork, try to provide clear evidence of how and when you have developed this skill.

Things you haven't had the chance to tell them about in other parts of the form. If you have space, write about your leisure pursuits or interests. Although they may not be directly relevant to the job, you could have developed some pertinent transferable skills.

Finally, make sure you end your statement positively, for example, you could use the final paragraph to reinforce your motivation and commitment. Keep to any word count and check your spelling and grammar – recruiters will be looking for evidence of your written communication skills. Customize your application to the organisation or institution you are applying to. Show enthusiasm as to why you want the job or course. Meet the essential criteria. Some recruiters will emphasize academic achievement whilst others will be looking for particular skills, knowledge and experience. Give complete answers and provide convincing examples.

Remember...

V – Values

I – Interests

P – Personality

S – Skills

TRICKS RECRUITERS USE TO FILTER APPLICATIONS

Don't cut corners. Don't be tempted to 'cut and paste' information and answers across from previous applications. Employers can usually tell when this is done as your answer won't exactly match the question that they asked. Even worse, applicants sometimes leave the previous organisation's name or a different course title in the application! You can use a previous application as a prompt but write a new answer for each question.

Take plenty of time over the application. A good application takes a long while to complete and rushing an application will simply be a waste of your time. It might take you a whole day to complete your first application form but hopefully, your efforts will be rewarded with an interview or an offer on a course!

Create A Personal Brand

→ Your talents – focus on what you do well

- Your values - what's important to you
- Your USP – talents and values along with experience and career aims

HOW TO HANDLE REJECTIONS

Once, I was rejected for an internal position. Wow, unbelievable, I said to myself. I felt dejected and worthless at the same time. However, I didn't just let it slide, as this rejection affected my confidence level and I can't let it go.

Few days down the line, this rejection impacted my performance at work. Three weeks after, I learned about the reason I was rejected.

The reason I was rejected is this: The other candidate presented a better argument involving a combination of both his skills, qualifications and accomplishments backed up with compelling storytelling from what he has done in the past.

This is where my journey to researching the competency-based interview began. For ten (10) years, I researched the evidence-based interview (behavioural/competency-based interview).

Since learning about this secret, I haven't failed any job interview again.

Whether the rejection comes at the application form stage or after an interview, it's disheartening and can have an impact on your confidence, especially if it happens a few times. The first thing to remember is that many others are in the same position. You should contact the company by sending them an email within a week of the rejection, politely thanking them for their time and asking that they retain your details for any future opportunities. Ask what you did well and where your application fell, as this can help you approach the next one more confidently.

If you're struggling to get to the interview stage you need to develop an action plan of achievable mini-goals such as:

- Improve your CV
- Gain extra work experience
- Use social media to job hunt
- Hire a coach or consult with an expert in the field
- Meet and connect with new people in the field

Having come to the end of this chapter, the next chapter will be focusing on Competency-based Interview Question and Answer.
This section will equally show you how to structure your answer with positivity even if your experience was a negative result.

CHAPTER FIVE

This section will give you an example to best answer the competency-based interview questions with the STAR, C.A.R.L and P.A.R.L model/technique with real-life and hands-on examples, drawing inference from the author's experiences.

See you in the next section!

THE COMPETENCY-BASED INTERVIEW Q&A

◆ ◆ ◆

Competency-based Questions & Answers with Real life and hands-on Examples:

1) **Tell me about yourself?**

Best way. I am Blessing Nkechi Ikiseh. I have twelve years of experience in the nonprofit, academia and corporate sectors and earned my Bachelor of Science degree in Business Administration from Lagos State University, Nigeria. I completed my Masters of Science degree in Business Psychology with the University of South Wales, United Kingdom. The reason for choosing this field/work stems from an intellectual curiosity to understand human behaviour psychology to workplace settings, business and daily living.

As the Human Resource Manager for a recent organisation (MGON), I have developed a range of systems to increase the efficiency of the human resource practices of the organisation, which include conducting a mini communication audit report to ascertain the communication among all levels of staff. The result indicated various changes needed to be made in the communication structure of the organization which were then successfully implemented, thus recognized by Senior Leadership for my problem-solving and conflict management skills.

Previously, I worked with a nonprofit organisation to develop and implement systems to create a more efficient method of storing and retrieving information through the production of an organized information structure.

I have volunteered as a Career Development Specialist/Training Facilitator for several nonprofit and education management institutions and groups, including NDGS and SFFG in Nigeria. Through these experiences, I developed a strong passion for social change. This passion birthed the initiative **'Bibieandrea Services Venture'**.

In my current portfolio as an HR Advisor/Organisational Psychologist, I help coach organisational and HR leaders, and executives to become better leaders.

I am highly skilled in Human Resources Management, Recruitment, Project Management, Training and Education, Research and Development, etc. I have worked hard to ensure that the vision and mission of the institutions/organisations I have worked with are implemented.
I am confident that my array of experience and skills will be mutually beneficial to both I and XYZ organisation.

❖ ❖ ❖

2) Why do you want to work for us? Or why should we hire you for this job?

Keynote. In this question, all the interviewer(s) wants is to state your name, your job role, your key job accomplishments and your skills, aligning them with the job position of the company you applied for, showing how you are bringing the result to increase the organisational productivity of the company.

Best way. Throughout my professional career, I have demonstrated exemplary levels of leadership service which has seen me volunteer for several groups including NDSS, SFCC and St. Francis Board of Lectors in Nigeria.

Through these experiences, I developed a strong passion for social change in the domain of youth development and education. This passion birthed the initiative *Bibieandrea Services Venture*.

I believe strongly in a world where everyone regardless of your age, race, social status, sexual orientation, political affiliation, etc. can come together to create a sustainable, just and a fairer world free from prejudice, promoting cultural diversity and inclusive society and that is what XYZ is about. XYZ organisation offers an excellent opportunity for social change leaders to network and to create valuable global change-makers contact.

Besides, I am a strong fit for XYZ Company whose mission strongly aligns with my long-term goals and career plan.

In this answer, the author tried to combine what XYZ Company is into. First, she demonstrated her exemplary levels of leadership service. XYZ Company is known for its service and volunteering work. Secondly, she stated the diversity and inclusion policy of XYZ which made her love what they do (which is accommodating everyone regardless of their religion or race). The author equally made mention of how they offer an excellent opportunity for social change leaders and last, of all, aligning XYZ mission to her career plans and lifelong goal.

3) Tell me about a time you experienced a new work culture and how did you handle it?

Keynote. This question is best suited if you are applying to a job abroad or far away from your location and/or if you are relocating to a new area.

Best way. While working as the Internal Consultant on a six months contract for NDSS in Benue State, Nigeria, I had travelled from Lagos State, Nigeria for this job. Noticing the diversity of the new work culture, I handled the situation using observational skills to decide each person's gestures by communicating effectively what I mean. I appreciate our differences both in culture and tradition. I was open to learning a new culture and environment, thus, appreciated our cultural diversity.

4) Tell me a time you disagreed with a team member and how did you handle it?

Best way. Just recently, I disagreed with a team member concerning our 2020 training programme for Bibieandrea Services Venture. My Business Manager had suggested we continue with our usual training programme using the same strategy. I carefully listened to her concerns and her thought process to learn something new from her ideas. After suggesting how the training programme should take place, I didn't quite agree with her plan. I asked her what her concerns would be if we did this differently by introducing a certificate of participation to give out to each participant after every event. She gave her reasons as to why this isn't entirely a good idea and how we needed to save cost. We arrived at a compromise, we agreed that instead of printing out every certificate to give out to each participant, we decided to email a Pdf copy of each participant's certificate to them. I believe the experience helped me improve my conflict management skills.

5) Tell me a time you encountered a difficult situation at work? Or tell me a time you used different leadership styles or five leadership styles to solve a problem?

Best way. As the Human Resource Manager for a recent organisation (MGON), I was working with three (3) of my colleagues to beat a deadline on an HR policy proposal we were drafting.

Two (2) of my colleagues didn't quite agree with each other on how to approach the project proposal. It was obvious we needed to work better as a team.

During lunchtime at work, we were able to openly discuss the details of the project proposal, allowing both to hear the full scope of each other's plans.

Having lunch together gave them the opportunity that they have similar ideas but disagreed on smaller and less significant details.

After hearing each other's plans, we made a single list using the best and the most relevant ideas we all agreed on. In all, we had a single list for our HR policy proposal draft and the Senior Management were happy.

I believe the experience helped me work better as a team while growing in my leadership, conflict management, communication, collaboration and listening skills.

Keynote. After telling a compelling story on the difficulty encountered, the author equally showed how her skills improved. The learning objective of question five (5) emphasizes leadership, team building and collaboration skills. As such, the author used collaborative skills, conflict management and listening skills to arrive at a solution. Drawing on the inference between transformative, transparent and participatory leadership styles that were used to proffer solutions to the conflict/difficulty encountered at work.

6) Please select two XYZ values and describe how you actively engage with those values in your professional life?

Best way. The two XYZ values I actively engage within my professional life are service to a cause greater than yourself and Empathy.

I have often lived a life of selfless service, dedication and commitment, which has seen me done more than my fair share of the work on projects while working in teams. As an aside, to empathize with my clients and colleagues, I first learn and care about their lives.

By observing what my clients/colleagues do and how they interact with their environment, gives me a glimpse of how they think and feel.

Using this strategy, I have been able to learn first-hand the motivation behind their human behaviour.

By engaging with my clients/colleagues and the people I encounter daily, reveals to a great extent the values they uphold.

> Jim Stovall supports this when he quotes "You need to be aware of what others are doing, applaud their efforts, acknowledge their successes, and encourage them in their

pursuits. When we all help one another, everybody wins".

This is how I manage to build strong teams to manage teams with exceptional performance, using integrity in relationship building.

Keynote. XYZ organisation has seven (7) values they uphold. From the question, the author was asked to select two values and she selected the values of Empathy and Selfless service signalling that she has used these throughout her professional life. These values align with the values of XYZ Company. At the end of the story, the author also showed how she has used integrity to build healthy relationships with her clients/colleagues. XYZ Company is also known for their values of integrity and relationship building.

7) **Learning from mistakes is part of professional development, and strong leaders can effectively handle challenges. Describe a specific instance when you made a mistake or encountered a setback that helped you grow as a leader. What did you do and how are you applying those lessons learned in your current work?**

Best way. In 2015, I ventured into a fashion accessory business. This start-up failed as a result of using the out of pocket money to initially fund the business without setting a prior business model. I learnt the lesson of having a well-defined business model for any project I want to establish. I underwent a training certification course on Business Management and Entrepreneurship that taught me the strategies of creating a concrete business model as a business owner. This strategy has helped me grow as a leader. Since the inception of Bibieandrea Services Venture in 2018, I have applied the strategy learnt in my previous failed project by setting up an appropriate model. Also, I have applied the strategy of using debt finance mainly to expand the project and not when starting it up, but rather start small or pool resources through partnership.

8) How do you build relationships?

Best way. First, I extend a hand of friendship by taking a genuine interest in other people. I make it all about the people I encounter daily by showing interest in their work and daily lives. Secondly, I make it easy for people to get along with me by being patient, generous and attentive with my time. Finally, I am very generous at encouraging people. I listen, motivate and inspire them by being prepared to show affection, giving advice or by counselling them. I put plenty of energy into creating a cordial environment where everyone feels at ease. I carry forward this attitude in my everyday life because I feel that creating a healthy and encouraging environment for people both on and off work makes them more productive, which creates a mutual feeling of trust, honesty and reliability.

9) Why should our organisation select/hire you over other candidates?

Keynote. This is a two and/or 3 minutes pitch explaining why you stand out from everyone else. The key here is to talk about your unique selling point, your key job accomplishments and how you are a result-driven individual. In the end, all employers like the result. Show how you are bringing your result-driven skills to solve problems for the organisation.

Secondly, show how working at their company will fit into your career plan because of what they do or produce and/or how you are a big fan of the company. Make sure you are genuinely interested in the job and will be motivated to perform if hired. Compare your professional goals with the objectives of the company and the position. Briefly explain your key professional job accomplishments/results. Even though the question is about why you want to work there, you still need to show or convince the interviewer that hiring you will benefit the company.

Best way. The reason XYZ organisation should select me over other candidates is that I am a lifelong learner. I have learned agility. I take what I have learnt and translate it into a new situation. I believe that a person who is adaptable, flexible and open to learning is far better than a person who is not open to learning. Because of my lifelong learning and adaptability skills, I have been an asset to every employer, which has seen me created several systems to improve the working methods of every organisation I have worked with including spearheading the development of a school's human resource department to increase the efficiency of storing and retrieving information for a more organized information structure.

This speaks to my overall intellect and ability to learn to serve better.

I am accountable for results and this will make me an even greater asset to XYZ Company.

What makes me stand out from everyone else is that I am a person of execution. This has seen me done more than my fair share of the work on projects working in teams. This is my method of getting things done faster than most. I am known for my mantra of speed and commitment to organisational results.

I have a very strong background in Programme/Project Management, Business Psychology/Consulting, Strategic Human Resources Planning, Training and Education, Research and Development, but also about encouraging, motivating and inspiring people to get the work done. I believe that it drives personal accountability, develops and grows people and ultimately, leads to better organisational results.

I am a Human Resource Advisor/Organisational Psychologist that has a positive impact on companies. Having been recognized by senior leadership for all the organisations I have worked in for my problem solving and conflict management skills, being asked to complete a task dealing with disruptive situations ensuring that a suitable resolution was attained to minimize disorder.

I am very good at what I do, and I get things done because I create a path that is directed and focused on results, I am a problem solver. I am truly excited to have the opportunity to work with XYZ organisation.

10) What will you be doing when you return to your home country?

Keynote. This question is appropriate if you have applied for a job or a fellowship abroad that requires you to come back to your home country and teach the skills learnt in your community.

Best way. Returning to my home country, I will continue the work I am doing of empowering the youths and professionals with the necessary tools to grow and develop in their field of choice. Applying an experience working abroad returning home, I will share the skills learnt, the effective practices, the worthwhile experiences, by establishing a network of valuable global change-makers contact. This will enable me to stay abreast of the latest development in my field.

Applying the knowledge and experience acquired through the XYZ Fellowship, in my home country, I would have been equipped with the needed tools to engender change and innovation, which will go a long way in equipping the unemployed youths and the educationally disadvantaged persons in society.

11) Tell me a time you led a team and how did you handle it?

Best way. One time, while working as the Internal Consultant for DNGS, I was contacted on secondment by my former employer

(SSFC) to diagnose the institution's ineffective leadership management.

Spearheading this project while working with a team of ten (10), the following was recommended to increase the human resource practices of the school which were then successfully implemented.

We diagnosed the problem of the school to be the lack of structure and the inadequate training and development of staff.

We created the following systems:

- Developed the school's primary human resources department increasing the efficiency of storing and retrieving information.
- We developed the institution's semester budgets and established an accounting system to create a more efficient method of income/expenditure management.
- We suggested several leadership interventions programmes for the institution including adequate training and development of staff, and proper motivational policy structure.

I believe that the experience helped me to improve my leadership abilities while growing in my consultancy, collaboration and people management skills.

12) Tell me about a time you had to work with a difficult person? This question can also be asked as tell me about a time you have used five types of skills to solve a problem and how did you handle it?

Best way. I was working with a team of Ten (10) as nominated head of the event planner for SSFS when I noticed that a team member was not deadline conscious. He joked about every little thing when we needed to be serious.

Resolving the situation, I sat him down and talked to him to see if he needed any help and where I needed to assist him with his duties. After talking with him, he explained his concerns to me that he had become stressed out trying to do his duties to meet the deadline and that joking around was his method of easing out stress. He apologized and informed me he didn't know that his action was distracting the team. I told him to take 15 minutes to break to ease off his stress levels and then come back to his duties.

I am happy I was able to help ease the stress levels of a team member thereby growing in my leadership, communication, conflict management, feedback and listening skills.

13) Describe a time when you received criticism?

Best way. As the Human Resource Manager for MGON Company, I train and develop staff and assist them to grow their careers both personally and professionally. At the end of each training session, I always send out surveys about how to improve the training session of the company to better assist employees based on needs. I received some valuable criticisms from employees. Some of the key criticisms include that the organisation should improve its communication structure and this can benefit the employees in the long run.

I quickly took the constructive criticism to mind and suggested to the senior management the importance of effective communication at all levels. I was fortunate to conduct a mini communication audit report for MGON to ascertain the communication among all levels of staff, the result indicated various changes needed to increase the communication channels of the organisation which were then successfully implemented.

This experience helped increase my communication skills and my ability to entertaining feedback through constructive criticism.

14) **How do you deal with stress?**

Before giving you the best way to answer this question, I want you to think about a time you were:

  i. Faced with a deadline at work

  ii. You had a conflict at work

  iii. You resolved a conflicting situation at work

  iv. You encountered difficult clients at work

   v. You were doubling between your job and a co-workers job

   vi. You volunteered to take up a job/task alongside your work schedule

Think about these scenarios from your experience.

This question is also known as:

  a. How do you handle work pressure?

  b. How do you handle conflict?

  c. How do you handle occupational stress?

  d. How do you deal with work stress?

  e. How do you manage stress?

In This Question

The interviewer wants to know how you handle stress by digging deeper into your personality. Make sure to tell the interviewer(s) that:

You perform at your best and enjoy working under pressure conditions.

You manage stress and pressure by being organized in your work.

You prepare for any eventuality by adopting a good time management policy and work balance.

Tell the interviewer that you manage stress so well by concentrating on the task at hand.

Say you manage stress so well by promoting healthy living and keeping yourself healthy and fit because this helps increase your concentration levels.

Ultimately, give an example of when you have previously worked under stress or pressure and how you managed/handled it.

I will give you two examples of how to manage/deal with stress at work.

Best way. I prefer to work under stress/pressure conditions; this is when I am at my best. I deal with stress by focusing on the task at hand. I remain calm by creating to-do lists and in what order. For example, one time, a colleague called in sick. My supervisor needed a volunteer to carry out her work while she was absent. I volunteered to take up the task. To make sure I deal with the stress of doubling up with two jobs, I obtained a clear brief from my supervisor. I created a list of what needed to be done and by what timescale to manage my time. I focused intently on each task without any distractions. I was able to do this by keeping fit, eating, exercising and staying healthy. By engaging in these activities, it enables me to maintain optimum concentration levels whilst at work.

Put another way. As the Senior Accountant for XYZ Company, I was promoted to the Chief Administrative Accountant, while also doubling as the Human Resource Manager. I dealt with the stress that came up with these positions by remaining calm - focusing intently on each task without any distractions. I adopted a good time management policy through individual goal setting, by creating a to-do list and prioritizing the relevant job first. I set boundaries that involve effective techniques. For example, I take my work breaks very seriously. I take short vacations and eat breakfast. Knowing how stress can negatively impact work performance and organisational productivity and resources, I take preventive measures by managing my time, keeping fit and healthy to maintain maximum concentration whilst at work.

15) Present yourself - tell us about your motivation for this position/working at XYZ and give three previous examples of your past activities/involvements relevant to this position?

Before we dive deeper into the best way, I want you to think about your reason for applying:

Think about your job accomplishments.

Think about any awards or recognition you have, if any, etc.

Use your cover letter, your CV/resume and job duties submitted for the job to come up with the best answer from your experience.

The Motivation For Applying

This question can equally mean:

1. Why should we hire you for this role?

2. Why are you the best candidate for this position? Do not say you are the best candidate. Say you are the right candidate.

3. Why should we select you over another candidate?

Keynote: The best candidate from a pool of job applicants may not necessarily be the right candidate for the job. Knowing the right candidate is where competency-based interviewing comes into place. Competency-based interview questions let you talk. They are open, inviting you to respond, telling the employer about real-life challenges that you have faced – backed up with a compelling story of how you solved the problem.

Structuring your answer with positivity even though the result is negative - the way you respond is the game-changer to standing out from your peers. Finally, let your personality shine in this question.

Best way. My name is Blessing Nkechi Ikiseh. I am an Organisational Psychologist. I am motivated to work for XYZ because I have excellent analytical skills and a willingness to learn. At XYZ, I will learn new skills, which means I am continually improving to serve better. I enjoy the thrill of completing challenging tasks when I am under pressure. I also love giving good service to clients - this makes me feel proud that I am making a positive impact on their day. I have 12 years of experience in leadership in a variety of settings.

For example:

In my current portfolio working for Bibieandrea Services Venture, I support the educationally disadvantaged people and empower youth through quality education. Through this initiative, I have partnered with academic and education management institutions to provide quality education and empower the educationally disadvantaged people for over 2,000 Nigerians. I have also provided grants to out-of-school children in my home country. I enjoy working alongside other management professionals to ensure customers receive the most appropriate care for their needs.

I also have experience working to maintain my professional competence - I am aware of this while working for (MGON) on the significance of employee training and development including new hire orientation, leadership training and professional development.

Besides, as a Human Resource/Administrative Assistant at SFSS, I developed and managed budgets working in collaboration with team members to reduce expenses by 30%. My main activities were related to Human Resources Management. I have experience demonstrating all leadership values in my work. My experience qualifies me as the right candidate for the position of Human Resource Generalist. I am excited to work with XYZ.

Keynote. Tell the interviewer your EXPERIENCE is a match for the job description and you are the right candidate for the position/role. If the interviewer(s) is aware you have studied the job description, it will inform them you are serious about the position; and you have taken steps to prepare for this role/position.

Tell the interviewer that your experience entails:

1. Working under pressure
2. Effective communication
3. Team working
4. Problem-solving

Tell the interviewer your experience means they won't spend time supervising you - you have everything you need to do the job.

17) Leaders can achieve progress despite differing views or identities. Please explain a situation where you have worked with people from different backgrounds, identities or perspectives of your own and had to use your leadership skills to resolve

a conflict or disagreement with others. What actions did you take? How did you encourage respectful discussion?

Best way. A conference conducted by the Body of Corporations in early January 2019, which had 250 participants from 25 firms, gathered to deliberate on a project entitled "The Causes of Reduced Workers Productivity and Incentives: A Case Study of Sub-Saharan Corporations".

Eighty-two (82) research participants were in disagreement on one of the formulated hypotheses. The following are the actions taken to encourage respectful discussion:

Through the use of peaceful collaboration and effective communication, I informed the participants of the benefits of the project to their corporation.

I provided a framework for debate by creating a structured approach different sectors can adopt for resolving internal and external work crises.

Finally, I provided a structure through which African leaders can collaborate to create policy reforms to solve challenges.

I learnt the importance of listening to people and seeing their points of view. Thus, my communication, conflict and collaboration skills improved.

In conclusion, use these job interview examples to your advantage by telling a compelling story about your experiences, skills and achievements.

CHAPTER SUMMARY

IN RETROSPECT

Chapter one (1) of this book discussed the competency-based interview and its meaning while learning about your background and the experience relevant to the competencies being accessed. Besides, you learned about the pros and cons of the competency-based interview.

Chapter two (2) explained the competency-based interview questions in more detail, giving relevance to the various types of competency-based interview technique.

Chapter three (3) focused on how the competency-based interview questions are scored, both their positive and negative indicators, citing also, the thirty (30) most common competency-based interview questions.

In chapter four (4), you learn about the basic application principles; the type of questions you are likely to get asked at the interview; how to spot the ATSs and dealing with gaps in your CV/resume.

Chapter five (5) discussed at length the competency-based interview questions and answers, citing real-life and hands-on experience, drawing inference from the author's experiences.

RECOMMENDATION

Dear Professionals,

Remember, the job interview is a two-way street, when done right, can turn into an engaging conversation between the candidate and the interviewer(s), and by this, you will be one step ahead of your peers.

In my 12 years of experience as an HR Practitioner/Recruiter and counting, I have learned that even the most qualified and exceptional candidates, fail to stand out by asking hard-hitting - yet thoughtful and engaging questions.

These are four (4) questions I wish more candidates had the confidence to ask during the job interview.

1. What are the biggest obstacles I will encounter within 90 days, and how will you measure success?
2. How does my background compare to other candidates you are interviewing?
3. Reflecting on your experience, what have you seen the

organisation do to promote diversity, equity and inclusion?
4. What have I said or not said that might lead you to believe I am unsuitable for the job?

Bonus: What can you tell me about the make-up of the team I will be working with?

The fourth question will help you get immediate feedback about the interview and your performance.

The interviewer(s) response will better assist you to understand how purpose-driven the company is and if their career values align with yours.

PRACTICE THE FOLLOWING QUESTIONS

1. Why do you want to leave your current job or position?

Key Tip. The reason for wanting to leave my current job role is that this job will give me an excellent opportunity to further advance my adaptability, flexibility and lifelong learning skills, Besides, provide me with enhanced career advancement and professional development opportunities.

2. Why do you want to work for us?

Key Tip. Show how working at their organisation will fit into your career plan because of what they produce or the service they offer to the public. Show how you are a big fan of the organisation. Be certain that you are genuinely interested in the job and will be motivated and inspired to perform if employed.

Compare your professional goals with the objectives of the firm and the job role. Briefly explain your professional job accomplishments/results.

3. Where do you see yourself in the next ten (10) years from now?

Key Tip. Describe your job role, your passion, the projects you have worked on and/or currently working on and how these accomplishments, projects and goals fit around your lifelong goals and career plans and explaining how that of the organisation's vision, mission, goals and purpose strongly aligns with yours.

4. What makes you want to work hard?

Key Tips. Talk about the passion you have for the job, how committed, dedicated and selfless you are and the skills you have used in all the organisations you have worked for. Show how these skills have become part of your daily mantra.

5. What are your long - term career goals?

Key Tip. Question three (3) and question (5) are strongly related only in that this speaks about your long term goals which can also be your long term career plans/vision.

6. How confident are you that you can successfully perform the duties of this position and why?

Key Tip. Tell a compelling story about how you have brought about results in all your previous and/or current employment. Talk about any awards you have been given in your job roles and wrap it up with key quantifiable achievements. Finally, show how confident you will be to execute this job role using the same strategy you have used in all your recent/current positions to be successful in this job role.

7. Describe a situation that would exemplify your integrity?

Key Tip. Pick two of the organisation's values and describe how these values resonate with you and your integrity and show how you have applied these values in all your work environment to lead the way of a person with integrity. Remember, tell a compelling story.

8. Tell me a time you led a project while working with a team?

Key Tip. While there is no right and wrong answer to this question, there is the best way.
Start by talking about:

1. The time you were working for a recent or current organisation and the position you were handling.

2. Tell the interviewers how many people you are working with while spearheading this project.

3. Explain the problem you and your team were resolving.

4. In details and concisely, explain the recommendation or the outcome of the project.

P.S. The result can be either good or bad, negative or positive. There is no need to beat yourself up. Learning from the mistake is part of professional development.

5. The suggestions you and your team gave were it successfully implemented by the organisation?

6. What did you learn from this experience?

Remember, use the 'STAR' technique to answer these questions.

OTHER QUESTIONS TO LOOK OUT FOR

❖ ❖ ❖

Describe a situation you led a team?

❖ ❖ ❖

Give an example of a time you handled conflict in the workplace?

❖ ❖ ❖

Tell me about a time you achieved success when the odds were stacked up against you?

❖ ❖ ❖

Tell me a time you beat the deadline at work?

❖ ❖ ❖

Give an example of a situation where you used creativity to solve a problem?

❖ ❖ ❖

Tell me about a time you decided on a decision and changed your mind?

❖ ❖ ❖

What method do you use to motivate your team?

❖ ❖ ❖

Tell me about a time when your communication skills improved a decision?

❖ ❖ ❖

Describe a project where you used different leadership styles to reach your goal?

❖ ❖ ❖

Tell me about a project you led that failed?

❖ ❖ ❖

How much salary should we pay you?

❖ ❖ ❖

Tell me a time you disagreed with your boss?

❖ ❖ ❖

Tell me a time when you had a difficult situation?

❖ ❖ ❖

Tell me about a time when you were part of a failing team?

❖ ❖ ❖

Tell me a time you demonstrated leadership skills?

◆ ◆ ◆

How do you handle receiving feedback?

◆ ◆ ◆

How would you communicate the implementation of performance measurements so as not to panic a staff under your supervision?

Best way: Once, I had a tough conversation when I thought about the performance evaluation I will give one of our employees, Jude, sometime last year.

Jude has been with XYZ Company for two years, and over the last six months his performance has begun to slide.

As the manager, it is my responsibility to talk with him about performance, which I have done on several occasions. However, the performance evaluation will make his nonperformance more formalized. Although Jude has had some personal troubles that can account for some of the performance issues, despite this, I need to get his performance up to par. My goal in the performance evaluation interview today is to create an improvement plan for Jude while documenting his nonperformance.

When I arrive at work, I look over the essay rating part of Jude's evaluation, it details two client project deadlines that were missed, as well as the over-budget amounts of the two client projects. It was Jude's responsibility to oversee both aspects of this project. When Jude arrives at the office, I greet him, ask him to take a seat, and begin to discuss the evaluation with him. "Jude, has always been a high performer, these last few months have been lacklustre".

On two of the office projects, he was over budget and late. Clients commented on both of these aspects when they filled out the client evaluation. I can see this is documented in his performance evaluation."

"Ultimately, as the account director, I am responsible for your review, as outlined in your job description. As you know, it is important to manage the accountability within your team, and in this case, you didn't perform.
In fact, in your 360 reviews, several of your colleagues suggested you were not putting in enough time on the projects and seemed distracted."

I worked together with Jude to develop an improvement plan so he can continue to add value to the organization. The improvement plan addresses project deadlines and budgets, and he found it helpful for his career development. Jude agrees begrudgingly and I begin to show him the improvement plan document the company uses, so we can fill it out together. As I had suspected, he was defensive at first but seemed enthusiastic to work on the improvement plan after I showed him the document. I felt positive that this performance evaluation is the right direction to ensure Jude continues to be a high producer in the company, despite these mistakes.

◆ ◆ ◆

What means of communication may be used to effectively establish a new policy?

◆ ◆ ◆

What type of decision do you make in your current job?

❖ ❖ ❖

Describe a situation when your work was criticized and how you responded to the situation?

❖ ❖ ❖

What measures would you implement to encourage employee involvement in a quality improvement programme?

❖ ❖ ❖

Describe a situation when you are conducting a meeting and two participants are disrupting the meeting, what would you do?

TWENTY-FIVE TOP TRANSFERABLE SKILLS

1. Relationship building
2. Conflict Management
3. Adaptability
4. Communication
5. Time Management

6. Creativity and Innovation
7. Decisiveness
8. Compliance
9. Delegation and Collaboration
10. Empathy

11. Organisational and Planning Skills
12. Project Management
13. Reliability
14. Resilience and Tenacity
15. Risk-taking

16. Teamwork
17. Flexibility
18. Independence
19. Attention to details
20. Influencing, Inspiring and Motivating

21. Leveraging Diversity
22. Negotiation and Presentation Skills
23. Research and Development
24. Multi-tasking
25. Lifelong Learner.

We all have transferable skills, so identify them. For recent graduates use your University and internship placement skills (if any) as your transferable skills.

Your transferable skills must be showcased in the key skill section of your CV/resume and backed up with your quantifiable job achievements.

To Your Continued Success!

APPENDIX

BONUS

Tell me about a time you encountered a difficult situation at work and mention the types of skills you used to handle the situation?

Once, I was at a **'DILEMMA'**.

One of our best employees and top performer has recently begun to have some problems. He is showing up to work late at least twice per week, and he missed the mandatory employee meeting on Saturday. When I asked him about it, he said he is having some personal problems and informed me about his divorce crisis. His wife kicked him out of the house.

For a moment he got better, comes to work on time, and is his normal, pleasant self when helping customers. However, the situation gets more serious.

Two weeks later, the employee comes to work reeking of alcohol, smelling and wearing the same clothes he wore to work the day before.

Every day was a train wreck but he is still with us.

Do you know what made the difference? I decided not to let him fail. The team decided not to let him go. We stepped up to assist him with his duties. Now he is better and thriving. Life happens: We all have been there. We helped our colleague who is struggling. It could be us one day.

I used my Leadership, Human Resources, Teamwork, Motivation and inspirational skill sets to handle the situation.

EPILOGUE

Now that you know the secret of the competency-based interview and the basic application principle, start applying them to your advantage.

This book has been written to inspire confidence among professionals and I can categorically say the objective of the book has been achieved.

AFTERWORD

Here are five (5) deal breakers you shouldn't make during your job interview.

1. Giving unclear and indirect answers to straightforward questions.

Avoid telling irrelevant stories about your previous employer or being overly dramatic about how much you need the job.

2. You are more focused on questions regarding benefits and compensation.

Avoid sounding desperate only caring about "what's in it for you?" - employee benefits, salary, holiday allowance, working hours, etc., rather than "what are your expectations about this role and how can I serve you effectively?', you should take note.

3. Treating other employees you meet differently than they treat you.

Some candidates will be charming with whoever they perceive to be the hiring decision-maker but show a different side to others they meet.

4. Avoid complaining about your previous employers.

Stop playing the victim card.

5. You have obvious potential for job-hopping.

Employers want to hire somebody who will stick with them for the long-term, otherwise, you would only have to go through the hiring process again.

Finally, don't speak with a low tone during the interview. Be clear and speak audibly as possible. Remember, the interview is a two-way street. Ask the interviewer questions. Not asking at all will sound to the interviewer(s) as disinterested.

Having learnt from my recent experience, these are my top deal - breakers.

THE JOB DESCRIPTION IS A CRY FOR HELP

It's All In Your Mind!

Using the job description against yourself looks like this:

1. I don't check all these boxes
2. I don't have five (5) years experience
3. I can't do this job
4. I am not qualified
5. I don't have strong skills to stand a chance
6. They are looking for someone with more experience and better qualification
7. I need ABC qualification first before I consider applying for this role.

This thought makes you feel discouraged, which means, you won't apply and if you do, you are convinced it won't matter anyway.
You miss the information the job description is giving you with this mindset.

The job description is a source of data and facts that you collect and use to your advantage instead of against you.

a) It tells you what problems need to be solved.

b) It tells you why they are hiring for that job and why they are willing to pay someone to come in and help out.

c) It tells you what you do have and can bring to the table.

d) It gives you strategic information about what phase the company is in right now and why they need to spend on extra brain power.

A job description is a cry for help. Don't let a job description discourage you from getting your dream job.

You need to give yourself a chance first before someone else can take a chance on you.

If you struggle with believing you can't help, that is your real problem. The job description is just a word on a page that hiring managers arbitrarily decided would go there.
Don't let a job description discourage you from chasing after your dream job or career.
Don't let yourself shut down and forget all about your experience and capabilities.

The Job Description is a cry for help!

SURVIVING THE GLOBAL PANDEMIC: COVID HACKS TO STAYING MOTIVATED & ENCOURAGED

The impact of COVID-19 virus goes beyond mortality rates. The virus affected governments, private sectors, nonprofits, companies/businesses and even individuals around the world, which has seen governments globally prepare for contingency plans and aid packages to sustain their economies. Besides, every day, we hear worrying news of companies/businesses shutting down operations, announcing layoffs and employee pay cuts, which has seen a shift in the consumption patterns, resulting in shortages of goods and a hike in product prices in supermarkets and the grocery stores.

If you have lost your job due to the COVID-19 virus, don't get discouraged. The stress involved in losing a job can be draining and can take a toll on a person, relationships, physical, mental and emotional health.

Have you been forced to take early career retirement or see fewer contract offers? Stand firm, keep pushing, believing in yourself and your capabilities.

> Here are top ten tips to surviving if you have lost your job to COVID-19 global pandemic.

1. Develop your skills for personal and professional growth.

Due to the global pandemic, many education management institutions are given their training courses for free or at a discount. Now is the best time to take advantage of the opportunity. Developing, growing yourself for success and learning new skills is the way forward.

2. Always update your CV/Resume with the new skill.

By updating your CV/Resume regularly, it can better assist you with your career objectives/goals. It can also expose the gap in your CV and allow you to refocus your attention for personal and professional development.

3. Look at the loss of your job as temporary setbacks or think of it as a career break.

See this challenge as a way of learning from the experience and trying again.
What is your loss of job telling you? The feeling generated from losing a job can be easy to accept if you understand the lesson in your loss. Maybe losing your work has given you a chance to reflect on what you want out of life and rethink your career priorities.

4. Network your way to success.

LinkedIn is one of the best tools to look out for when seeking a career opportunity. Start looking for this opportunity by connecting with the people that matter most in your industry. The action you put on connecting with the right contact will be valuable if you are persistent, pessimistic and consistent. Your determinant spirit and perseverance will bring about all the work that will lead you to being successful.

5. The need to upskill, update your CV/Resume and prepare for job interviews is eminent.

Since there is a massive global layoff, when the economy settles downs and things return to normal, there is a 100% chance of massive recruitment.

Remember, success is a journey and it is limitless, but the desire and will to keep pushing is limited. With patience, determination, resilience and the right mindset, you will persevere.

Keep Pushing Until You Get To Your Required Destination!

MOTIVATION

Success is a journey and it is limitless, but the desire and will to keep pushing are limited!

Work on your goals a little bit every day no matter how small. The small efforts each day adds up to big results.

The goal is not to be successful, your goal is to be valuable and success will find you.

Your mindset is powerful! It can set you up for success, it can set you up to fail.

Procrastination is a thief of time!

Opportunities are never lost, someone will take the ones you have missed. Miss it, you might wait for a year or a lifetime.

Opportunities are not dressed in gold. They are dressed in overalls and look like work.

◆ ◆ ◆

It's All In Your Mind!

The only thing stopping you from achieving your goals or your dream is your mindset. Take Action Today.

ACKNOWLEDGEMENT

To him who has made this project work possible, God Almighty!

The author's sincere thanks go to all who in diverse ways has contributed invariably to the success of this study. Specifically, my sincere thanks go to the University of South Wales (USW), United Kingdom, and Kit Gerard Grant for their immense contributions, direction, and wealth of experience in the academic field that has made this project to be a success.

ABOUT THE AUTHOR

Blessing Nkechi Ikiseh

Blessing Nkechi Ikiseh earned her Bachelor of Science degree in Business Administration from Lagos State University, Nigeria. She completed her Master of Science degree with the University of South Wales School of Psychology and Therapeutic Studies, United Kingdom, majoring in Business Psychology. The reason for choosing this field stems from an intellectual curiosity to understand human behaviour psychology in workplace settings, business and for life. Blessing Nkechi Ikiseh is a social change person with different dimensions - author, social entrepreneur and researcher. She is the book author of An Employment Strategy Handbook and The Secret To Nail The Competency Based Interview: What You Need To Know. Blessing has 12 years of experience in the Nonprofit, Academia and Corporate Sectors. Through these experiences, she developed a strong passion for social change. This passion birthed the Training and Education initiative Bibieandrea Services Venture. As the Founder/CEO of Bibieandrea Services Venture, the project mission is to support the educationally disadvantaged people and empower youth through quality education in her community. Through her initiative, she has partnered with academic and education management institutions to provide quality education and empower youth and the educationally disadvantaged people for over 2,000 Nigerians. She has also provided grants to out-of-school children in her home country.

BOOKS BY THIS AUTHOR

An Employment Strategy Handbook

The recruitment and selection process of organizations bring about enhanced organizational and employee productivity. Selection is a technique used by organizations/businesses in choosing a suitable candidate for a job. Recruitment and selection involve a process which must pass a series of evaluation before final placement decisions can be made. The objective of this handbook is to identify how psychology plays an important role in ensuring reliable and valid psychological assessment in the workplace. This employment journal is borne out of scientific research and is based on employment screening, selection, placement and the interview process and it is written to help professionals, organizations and businesses better understand the recruitment and selection stages and the interview methods or processes used within organizations to better equip them to face the interview world while citing real-life and hands-on experiences (occurrence).

This book reviews the recruitment, employee selection, psychological assessment, the selection method, the reliability and validity of the selection assessment, the final selection and placement decision, the basic features of the interview, types of interviews, the interview formats, the interview contents and how the interview can be administered by an organization. Also, the journal answers some of the hard and not so hard interview questions while citing the best ways to answer them as it pertains to each person's knowledge, skills, past experiences and qualifications on the job. Stand Out From Your Peers And Be In Demand!

PRAISE FOR AUTHOR

This letter is a compliment to the reader for her work. It could be a direct tone with encouraging words for her efforts. You could be sincere without self-serving. Mention what exactly you love about this work. Appreciate the writer's good work.

- BLESSING NKECHI IKISEH

Thank you again, Blessing Nkechi Ikiseh. I was just offered a management role. I used your valuable information and questions to ask the interviewer to land the position.
I highly recommend this book - May 31 2021.

- VINESH K RAM

TESTIMONIAL

I found Blessing Nkechi on LinkedIn a few short weeks ago and I have not regretted working with her. She is being supportive, dependable and consistent with her passion and skills. I thoroughly enjoyed her coaching and I love my new CV which she worked on also her competency-based interview training book. Thank you, Blessing, for assisting me on my career development journey.

Amina A.

Blessing Nkechi I. is a mentor with a big mind and she is an educator with excellent coaching abilities. Blessing is dedicated, committed, determined and disciplined in her dealings. As a mentor, she has impacted a lot and she motivates and encourages professional development. She is open-minded and has forward-thinking abilities and also a very intelligent CEO, who has a lot of knowledge in her field and has exceptional expertise in leadership, coaching and motivation.

Benedict O.

Having worked with Blessing on multiple occasions, all of which contributed to the mutual growth of our companies and brand, I can truly say that she brings a ton of value to all projects that she engages with. Her tenure and experience in Human Resources and her expertise as a Psychologist are truly invaluable and her sincere desire to help, commendable.

Andrew V.

Blessing Nkechi Ikiseh is my mentor. I have benefitted so much from her mentoring and coaching services. I am excited at the steps she has taken just to see me succeed in my career.

Bojana P.

Blessing is an extraordinary and hardworking HR Practitioner and Psychologist, very motivational and insightful, open-minded, always eager to help and provide support. A great and inspirational person to be around. I am very glad for our cooperation.

Michal G.

Bibieandrea Services Venture is carving a niche in the quest for affordable, quality and sustainable education for educationally disadvantaged persons.

Patrick O.

Bibieandrea Services Venture is an excellent initiative, of which I am a beneficiary. Since Bibieandrea inception, the project has impacted, trained and engaged her community through its education and training programme.

David O.

Bibieandrea Services Venture is an excellent initiative, of which I am a beneficiary. It is set and continues to set the pace to provide affordable and quality education, entrepreneurial and human resources services to all those in dire need of it.

Victoria O.

Blessing Nkechi Ikiseh is a veteran in Human Resources. She goes the extra mile and does all that she can to make sure her clients are well prepared for any job interview (You should take a look at her handbooks (An Employment Strategy Handbook and the Competency-based Interview). I am humbled by the extra steps she has gone for me.

Victoria O.N

ABOUT BIBIEANDREA SERVICES VENTURE

Bibieandrea Services Venture was founded in 2018 and is into Education and Training of job seekers, students (both secondary and tertiary), prospective and existing entrepreneurs and professionals promoting innovation, collaboration and solutions by addressing the problem that arises from unemployment and poor quality education in her community.

Our mission is to give more out of school children in rural/peri-urban community access to quality education.

This project is providing the (tuition fees) to further two (2) out of school children education annually in her community. Also, our mission is to decrease the unemployment rate in graduates. This initiative has committed to training at least 300 youths annually in her community and beyond.

Since its launch, Bibieandrea has successfully supported six (6) out of school children education, one of whom is David, a 14-year-old out of school from South-West Nigeria and Cynthia a 15-year-old from the Eastern part of Nigeria.

Lastly, this initiative has successfully trained and impacted up to one thousand persons both onsite and virtually and secured a job for twenty (20) youths through her mentoring and coaching programmes; empowering youths with the necessary tools to grow and develop in their field of choice.

❖ ❖ ❖

Part of the proceeds of this book will be used to support the out of school children and/or the educationally disadvantaged people in her community.

OUR SERVICES

❖ ❖ ❖

Bibieandrea Services Venture Founded 2018

We are into Education & Training of job seekers, students, entrepreneurs and professionals.

Our mission is to give out of school children access to quality education and to decrease the unemployment rate in Nigerian graduates and beyond.

We provide services in the following field:

1. HR Consulting
2. Management Consulting
3. Business Consulting
4. How to leverage LinkedIn for busy professionals, businesses/companies
5. CV/Resume Writing
6. Cover Letter writing
7. LinkedIn Profile Writing
8. Business, Job Interview & Career Mentorship
9. Coaching Services
10. Academic Essay Coaching/Mentoring
11. Advising Companies

❖ ❖ ❖

Our project addresses the problem that arises out of unemployment and poor quality education by promoting innovation, collaboration and solutions through EDUCATION FOR SUSTAINABLE DEVELOPMENT (ESD).

Motto: Daring to be different by being the change that inspires others.

❖ ❖ ❖

Follow us on LinkedIn

https://www.linkedin.com/company/bibieandrea-services-venture

Printed in Great Britain
by Amazon